# A Room
# With a View

*by*
*Michael Patrick Allen*

# Contents

# Introduction

Few novels are more sceptical of guidebooks than *A Room With a View*. Some of E.M. Forster's characters are so caught up in reading about how to appreciate Florentine art and history they can hardly appreciate the present beauty of Florence in front of their eyes. Fortunately for the guide you are now reading, *A Room With a View* is also mistrustful of excessive scepticism about guides. A guide can perform the valuable service of making its reader stop and notice what he would otherwise pass by. This one aims to provide, in Forster's words, a few "different ways we can look at a novel".

The protagonist of *A Room With a View* is a young person in what one critic calls "the experimental season of life". As several generations of rapt readers testify, Forster provides Lucy Honeychurch with a compelling romantic (or courtship) plot: will she marry the passionate individualist, George Emerson, or the sardonic aesthete, Cecil Vyse? Or will she refuse to marry at all in order to make her own way through life? *A Room With a View* splendidly connects these urgent romantic questions with Lucy's equally urgent questions about her own self-development and place in the world. Lucy, as George Emerson's father notes, is in a "muddle". She struggles to live up to the ideals of her station in life until her encounter with the Emersons prompts her to question those very ideals. Then, Lucy must weigh the value of instruction against the value of experience, without yet having enough of either.

Obscurely dissatisfied with the narrow life that has been chosen for her, Lucy wishes for something to "happen to her". It does. She witnesses a murder at close hand and is rescued from a fainting spell by George Emerson. Afterward she tries to avoid him. By chance, she stumbles across him in a field of violets and he kisses her. Instead of clarifying her doubts about what she wants from life, these incidents throw Lucy into greater turmoil. Do the murder and the kiss prove the danger of stepping outside her narrow circle and its  standards of proper behaviour? Or are they evidence of "the call of the blood", a life of freedom and risks worth taking?

The passionate interest the other characters (and the reader) take in Lucy's choices is motivated by more than solicitude for her happiness. When Lucy finds the values of her set stifling, she implicitly condemns the code of propriety that props up the social position of her closest relations. When she chooses to marry for love outside her class, she implicitly rejects the narrow freedoms of respectable spinsterhood. Forster's candid and ironic narrator inserts himself into these debates. Like the novelists Henry Fielding and George Eliot before him, Forster gives the narrator permission to comment on the passions and misprisions of his characters. This intrusiveness irritated one of the novel's first reviewers. Forster, he wrote, "is full of views; what is worse, he is full of subtlety, a subtlety that rises up and assails you in pregnant epigram or paraded restraint".

The novel's views, or ideas, are presented with considerable subtlety and irony because, as Forster told a correspondent: "I can't write down 'I care about love, beauty, liberty, affection, and truth' though I should like to." *A Room With a View* is a novel of ideas. These ideas are intimately connected with the intrigue and suspense of Lucy's romantic plot. Yet the central drama of the novel is not to be found in murder or stolen kisses or proposals, but in Lucy's internal struggle to divide living from dead values. The novel is optimistic, not utopian on this score. The critic Lionel Trilling credits Forster with "a curious tough insight", and notes that "clear ideas are perhaps a sign of ignorance, muddle the sign of true knowledge".

# A summary of the plot

Part one of the novel begins with an overheard conversation. Charlotte Bartlett and her young cousin, Lucy Honeychurch, have just arrived in Florence. Over dinner, Charlotte complains that the proprietress of Pension Bertolini has given away their promised rooms "with a view". For her part, Lucy is disappointed to learn that the Bertolini, with its "Cockney" landlady and portraits of Lord Tennyson and Queen Victoria, hardly seems foreign. Charlotte, who delights in playing the martyr, insists that the next available room should go to Lucy. Their dispute is overheard by Mr Emerson, who is sitting nearby. He interjects himself without introduction into their conversation, saying: "I have a view, I have a view." Charlotte is as shocked by his offer as Emerson is baffled by her refusal to take it. Fortunately, Mr Beebe, an affable clergyman already known to Lucy and Charlotte, arrives in time to persuade Charlotte to overcome her misgivings.

Lucy and Charlotte are then introduced to the circle of English visitors around the Bertolini, all of whom come in for mild ridicule. The priggish Reverend Cuthbert Eager leads the English Church in Florence; the middle-aged Miss Alans are his dutiful parishioners. Miss Eleanor Lavish is a novelist who shocks and delights the other English visitors with her mild unconventionality. She offers to escort Lucy to the Basilica of Santa Croce, exhorting Lucy to leave her guidebook behind so she can experience "the true Italy". However, she abandons Lucy on the steps of the church to chase after "local colour" for her novel. Inside, Lucy falls in with Mr Emerson and his son George. They overhear Rev Eager lauding the faith and fervour of mediaeval art to his parishioners. Mr Emerson cannot help interjecting in favor of humanity and realism, though he is pained to discover he has "ruined the enjoyment" of Rev Eager's party with his interruption.

Mr Emerson believes his son is suffering from an existential depression. Lucy, he thinks, can convince his son to see value in living. Like her cousin Charlotte, Lucy is shocked by Mr Emerson's extreme candour. Back at the Bertolini, Lucy plays Beethoven on the piano in triumphantly expressive style. Mr Beebe reflects on the difference between her outwardly unremarkable demeanour and the passionate intensity of her playing. "If Miss Honeychurch ever takes to live as she plays," he reflects, "it will be very exciting."

Stirred by the Beethoven, Lucy sets out alone into Florence. She wishes for something to "happen" to her. After buying some photographs, she wanders into the Piazza Signoria where she sees one Italian murder another over a trifling sum of money. She faints from shock. When she returns to consciousness, George Emerson is supporting her in his arms. The murder and the embrace send Lucy into a panic. She attempts to slip away, but George insists on walking her back to the Bertolini. On their route, George suddenly throws her photographs – which are stained with the victim's blood – into the River Arno. He tells her that something more than the murder has happened. George concludes "I shall want to live" and Lucy hears an "unexpected melody" in the sound of the river.

Frightened by this intimacy, she attempts to avoid George. However, they are thrown together when the two clergymen arrange an outing to the countryside. The young Italian driving their coach is discovered canoodling with a young woman. Rev Eager and Mr Emerson quarrel over whether the driver should be punished. Lucy becomes separated from the rest of the party and goes in search of Mr Beebe. Forgetting the Italian word for clergyman, she asks the driver to direct her to "my good man". He takes her to a field overflowing with violets, where George Emerson kisses her. Charlotte sees them and tells Lucy that George is an ill-bred sexual adventurer who "takes a brutal pleasure in insulting a woman". The cousins depart the next morning for Rome.

The second part of the novel shifts to Windy Corner, the Honeychurch home in a Sussex village on its way to becoming a suburb. Lucy accepts the proposal of Cecil Vyse, whom she has previously twice rejected. Cecil, who is rich, clever, and well-connected, has conceived an aesthetic attraction to Lucy. She resembles, he thinks, the enigmatic women painted by Leonardo. Over the course of their engagement, Cecil grows increasingly irritated and, consequently, supercilious with Windy Corner and its inhabitants.

By chance, Cecil meets the Emersons in the National Gallery. Unaware of George's attentions to Lucy in Florence, Cecil puckishly arranges for the unconventional father and son to rent a "semi-detached" villa near Windy Corner in order to ruffle the sensibilities of the neighbourhood. Lucy's 19-year old brother, Freddy, takes George Emerson and Mr Beebe bathing in the "Sacred Lake" near Windy Corner. Lucy, out walking with Cecil, encounters the half-naked George Emerson for the first time since Florence. Freddy then invites George Emerson to a tennis party at Windy Corner. Cecil refuses to play in "public" so Lucy completes the foursome. As they play, Cecil mockingly reads aloud from an absurd novel. The novel, it transpires, is by Miss Lavish, writing under a pseudonym. Cecil obliviously reads aloud a chapter that describes a barely altered account of George and Lucy's kiss in the field of violets.

As they walk toward the house, George kisses Lucy again. Lucy falsifies her reaction to the event, denying her profound attraction to George. He confesses his love for her. Cecil stifles her spirit, he says, but "I want you to have your own thoughts even when I hold you in my arms". She refuses him, but is deeply affected by his appeal and immediately breaks off her engagement with Cecil. Having denied her head and heart, she prepares to join Charlotte in the "vast armies of the benighted... who have sinned against passion and truth".

Now eager to leave Windy Corner, Lucy arranges to travel to Greece with the Miss Alans. Mr Beebe approves of her determination not to marry, though her mother is pained by her increasing resemblance to Charlotte. Shortly before she is due to leave, Lucy encounters Mr Emerson in Mr Beebe's study. After she confesses to him that she has broken off her engagement to Cecil, Mr Emerson instantly sees that she loves George. She is in a "muddle", he tells her, and on the point of consecrating herself to a life of disappointment. Lucy is angry, then confused, and finally persuaded. In order to gather the strength to face her disapproving family, she kisses Mr Emerson.

George and Lucy marry. In the final chapter, they sit together in her old room in the Bertolini. Charlotte, they realise, knew Lucy would encounter Mr Emerson in Mr Beebe's study and allowed it to happen. Despite her surface antagonism to the match and repeated insistence that George is a cad, deep down she was on the side of love.

# Narration in *A Room With a View*

About half way through *A Room With a View*, Forster provides a wonderfully exaggerated example of the novel's key narrative technique:

*Playing bumble-puppy with Minnie Beebe, niece to the rector, and aged thirteen – an ancient and most honourable game, which consists in striking tennis balls high into the air, so that they fall over the net and immoderately bounce; some hit Mrs. Honeychurch; others are lost. The sentence is confused, but the better illustrates Lucy's state of mind, for she was trying to talk to Mr. Beebe at the same time.*

The passage is coloured by Lucy's state of mind, much as light appears coloured by the stained glass it passes through. The first sentence, as the narrator points out, is grammatically "confused". Like Lucy, it is distracted from its proper object: it consists of one long dependent clause that never arrives at its syntactically necessary subject and predicate. As readers, we are in Lucy's head, even if these are not exactly her words. Of course, *A Room With a View* employs the third person ("she"), not the first ("I"). Moreover, Lucy would have no reason to explain the rules of bumble-puppy nor to identify her playmate. Yet the manner of explanation and identification illustrate her way of thinking and feeling at the moment when she is playing bumble-puppy with Minnie.

This technique, often called "free indirect discourse", is usually more subtle in the novel than it is here. Take the first sentence of James Joyce's short story "The Dead": "Lily, the caretaker's daughter, was *literally* run off her feet". The intensifier "literally" is the sort of word Lily not Joyce would use. Hugh Kenner points out that "it is Lily, not the austere author [Joyce], whose habit it is to say literally when figuratively is meant". In *A Room With a View*, Charlotte Bartlett is usually referred to as "Miss Bartlett". Naturally, Lucy thinks of her as "Charlotte" and that is how she appears in third person descriptions particularly inflected by Lucy's consciousness, as in "Charlotte, with the complacency of fate, led her from the river to the Piazza Signoria".

Free indirect discourse is one important way that novelists manipulate point of view. Most of *A Room With a View* looks at the world from Lucy's perspective; it is really her story. However, more peripheral characters like Charlotte, Mr Beebe, Cecil, and even the coach driver, "Phaethon", sometimes assume centrality. The world looks different from their different standpoints. Crucially, the absence of Charlotte's perspective near the end of the novel allows Lucy and George to speculate about her unconscious affirmation of their love.

In *Aspects of the Novel*, Forster takes a principled stand against fixed rules of narration. Novelists, he writes, have no duty of consistency in the matter of point of view or the related matter of omniscience. The narrator's knowledge of his character's histories, motives, and fates is extremely elastic. Narration will, at times, inhabit a character's limited perspective on reality along with the particular emotional timbre of his point of view. For instance, the incongruous contents of the drawing room at Windy Corner – unstylish furniture and a bone from Freddy's medical studies – are described with peevish superiority because that is precisely how Cecil regards them. Then, for a moment, the view widens to emphasise the pitiable limitations of his perspective: "For Cecil considered the bone and the Maples' furniture separately; he did not realise that, taken together,

*Maggie Smith, Rupert Graves and Helena Bonham Carter in James Ivory's 1986 film adaptation of* A Room with a View

they kindled the room into the life he desired." "The right to intermittent knowledge," Forster writes in *Aspects of the Novel*, is one of the novelist's perquisites.

Joyce's alter ego, Stephen Dedalus, compares "the artist" to "the God of creation" who "remains within or behind or beyond or above his handiwork, invisible, refined out of existence, indifferent, paring his fingernails". In contrast, the narrator of *A Room With a View* is very often in the foreground. To be sure, the novel's narrator is not identical with its author; he is a fictional persona. Yet if he is a character in this limited sense, he is not known to the other characters nor implicated in the plot. The narrative theorist Gérard Genette calls this a "heterodiegetic" narrator and contrasts him with the "homodiegetic" narrator (like Nick Carraway in *The Great Gatsby*) who participates directly in the plot.

Like Forster himself, the narrator of *A Room With A View* is liberal-minded, cultured, ironical. He is not above gently correcting the whimsical Miss Lavish: "The men on the river were fishing. (Untrue; but then, so is most information.)" Nor does he refrain from moralising or making predictions. He believes, like Forster himself, in "Love, the beloved Republic" and the natural aristocracy of "the sensitive, the considerate and the plucky". When Lucy is on the point of giving up on love (and thus defecting from the beloved republic) in order to become a spinster, he foretells her doom:

> *She gave up trying to understand herself, and joined the vast armies of the benighted, who follow neither the heart nor the brain, and march to their destiny by catch-words. The armies are full of pleasant and pious folk. But they have yielded to the only enemy that matters – the enemy within. They have sinned against passion and truth, and vain will be their strife after virtue.*

Where Joyce's artist is impersonal and "indifferent", Forster's narrator evinces a personal and partial interest in the outcome of the plot he describes.

The implied readers of *A Room With A View* are made to feel that their rooting interest in George and Lucy's love places them among the aristocracy of "the sensitive, the considerate, and the plucky" instead of in the doomed ranks of "the army of the benighted" who "have sinned against passion and truth".

At times, Lucy stands in for the implied reader. She tells Charlotte that she kissed George in the field of violets because "for a moment he looked like someone in a book". And the same idea recurs to her when she encounters him, half-naked and in high spirits from swimming in the Sacred Lake (which itself takes its name from "some book").

Yet the incongruity between these moments of high literary romance and the prosaic attitudes and occupations of the Bertolini and Windy Corner does not go unremarked upon. The middle-aged Miss Alans, according to Mr Beebe, are looking for a room in a comfortable pension, and also a room with a view on to the "faery land" from John Keats's poem, "Ode to a Nightingale".

Eleanor Lavish is writing a "novel of modern Italy". Her pursuit of "local colour" and her fascination with sensation-charged novelistic material like murder and stolen kisses is the subject of deserved mockery. Nonetheless, her "dreadful novel" with its "draggled prose" produces the second romantic crisis at the conclusion of the book. No one could call Forster's urbane prose style draggled. Yet his novel is also "of modern

Italy" and relies on exactly the same murder and stolen kisses for its dramatic interest. There is thus a measure of self-satire in the self-referential parallels between *A Room With a View* and Miss Lavish's *Under a Loggia*.

# What is the significance of travel in the novel?

Early in *A Room With a View*, Mr Beebe reflects that "pension joys, pension sorrows, are flimsy things". These emotions are flimsy because a pension – a boarding house for travellers – is only a temporary society. Ostensibly, the guests' real lives are back in Britain; ostensibly, their real interests are the sights outside the wall of the pension. And yet, during his own tour of Italy Forster wrote "what a viewpoint is the English hotel or Pension! Our life is where we sleep and eat, and the glimpses of Italy that I get are only accidents." A pension is a semi-public place whose inmates have little power to invite or exclude. Persons separated at home by a fine mesh of class, taste and outlook are, in the temporary society of the pension, thrown together. There are limits to this mixing, of course. The guests of the Bertolini are a particular stratum of the middle classes: rich enough to travel, not so rich as to command their own establishments.

Still, the atmosphere is freer abroad. The

embarrassments and advantages produced by this freedom are a major theme of Forster's comedy of manners. In the pension, characters are thrown together before they can ascertain each other's class position. For instance, the inmates of the Bertolini comically misjudge the occupations of the Emersons. Miss Lavish takes Mr Emerson, a journalist, for a commercial traveller; Charlotte takes George Emerson, a clerk for a railway company, for a railway porter. The threat or charm of crossing class boundaries is especially felt by characters like Charlotte, whose primary asset is her claim to respectability. In England, Lucy accepted the way the boundaries of her set circumscribed respectability: "Outside it were poverty and vulgarity for ever trying to enter." Italy makes this social boundary feel arbitrary and surmountable:

> ...in Italy, where any one who chooses may warm himself in equality, as in the sun, this conception of life vanished. Her senses expanded; she felt that there was no one whom she might not get to like, that social barriers were irremovable, doubtless, but not particularly high. You jump over them just as you jump into a peasant's olive-yard in the Apennines, and he is glad to see you.

Such changes in one's "conception of life" are more permanent than the temporary society of the pension; therein lies their risk and promise.

Alongside the Bertolini's socio-economic hierarchy runs a hierarchy of travellers. Near the top, for Charlotte, are the English expatriates, like Mr Eager, who settle indefinitely in Florence:

*Mr. Eager was no commonplace chaplain. He was a member of the residential colony who had made Florence their home. He knew the people who never walked about with Baedekers, who had learnt to take a siesta after lunch, who took drives the pension tourists had never heard of, and saw by private influence galleries which were closed to them. Living in delicate seclusion, some in furnished flats, others in Renaissance villas on Fiesole's slope, they read, wrote, studied, and exchanged ideas, thus attaining to that intimate knowledge, or rather perception, of Florence which is denied to all who carry in their pockets the coupons of Cook.*

According to this view, residents in Florence, like Rev Eager, are the most immersed in local culture. The English colony takes on Continental habits, like the siesta, and Continental habitations. The English colony stands atop of a hierarchy of authenticity; participants in inclusive package tours like those Thomas Cook began offering in 1841 ("the coupons of Cook" were good for one meal or one overnight stay), are at the bottom.

The emphasis laid upon these distinctions of authenticity resulted from the democratisation of Continental tourism over the course of the 19th century. From the Early Modern Period to the 18th century, the Grand Tour provided the pattern for visitors to Italy. Young Englishmen of the upper classes visited France and Italy in order to refine their manners and encounter the remains of the classical world whose authors had formed the substance of their education in England. Samuel Johnson noted: "A man who has not been in Italy is always conscious of an inferiority." The Grand Tour was the culmination of education for the male elite. Its considerable expenses, including an entourage of tutors and servants, contributed to its prestige. For the Romantic generation of the late 18th and early 19th century, the sublimity and beauty of nature and its effect on the individual's sensibility vied with the glories of the classical past as an incentive to travel.

In the 19th century, innovations like the railway and the guidebook, pioneered by John Murray in England and Karl Baedeker in Germany, opened tourism to mass participation. Guidebooks offered those excluded by sex and class from a classical education a portable and inexpensive form of expertise, a substitute for the tutors who would accompany a wealthy young man on his Grand Tour. Travellers like Lucy Honeychurch simply referred to Baedeker, the omitted article suggesting a nearly human intimacy. This successful condensation of knowledge about sites of natural beauty and historic import into "Baedeker" inevitably raised the question of what precisely the tourist gains merely by *seeing* what he has already read expertly *described*.

Edith Wharton, writing in 1905, describes the predicament with a pictorial metaphor:

> *The foreground is the property of the guide-book and of its product, the mechanical sight-seer; the background, that of the dawdler, the dreamer and the serious student of Italy.*

This yearning after subjective and individual experience motivates Miss Lavish's animus towards guidebooks. "I hope we shall soon emancipate you from Baedeker," she tells Lucy. "He does but touch the surface of things." Miss Lavish prefers to "drift" confusedly through Florence instead of using maps, to search out authentic local colour instead of Baedeker-approved sights. Lucy, like the Emersons, finds the guidance of Baedeker useful rather than obtrusive. Despite its authority, she can still discover in herself a preference for terra-cotta babies over Giotto frescos. As Edward Mendelson writes in an illuminating article on the history of the Baedeker guides, their readers included "many thousands who combined within themselves a romantic personality and a bourgeois character".

# Why does Lucy break off her engagement because Cecil won't play tennis?

Cecil twice refuses to make up a tennis foursome. This, Lucy tells him, made her realise she must break off their engagement. Why does Cecil refuse and what does his refusal signify?

Though this exchange occurs in a chapter titled "Lying to Cecil", it is the truest reason Lucy offers for rejecting him. What does Cecil's refusal to play tennis indicate about his character? Lucy is the last person to realise that Cecil simply does not play well with others. Mr Beebe, who recognises in Cecil a kindred spirit, notes that "he's like me — better detached"; Freddie says "Cecil was the kind of fellow who would never wear another fellow's cap"; and George leads Lucy to her realisation when he tells her that Cecil "should know no one intimately, least of all a woman".

The narrator sums up their intuitions by identifying Cecil as a type:

> *He was medieval. Like a Gothic statue... he resembled those fastidious saints who guard the portals of a French cathedral. Well educated, well endowed, and not deficient physically, he remained in the grip of a certain devil whom the modern world knows as self-consciousness, and whom the*

*medieval, with dimmer vision, worshipped as*
*asceticism. A Gothic statue implies celibacy, just as*
*a Greek statue implies fruition...*

Lucy breaks off the engagement when she detects Cecil's ascetic detachment. "I am against asceticism myself," Forster said in his essay, "What I Believe". "Bodies are the instruments through which we register and enjoy the world."

*A Room With a View*, like all of Forster's novels, abounds in contraries: Gothic vs Greek, celibacy vs fruition, self-consciousness vs direct desire, inside vs outside. Lucy tells Cecil: "When I think of you it's always as in a room." George Emerson represents the positive side of all these oppositions. When she thinks of George, she recalls the beautiful view full of violets where they first kiss. When she first sees him again in England, he bows to her, half-naked in the joyous pagan atmosphere of the Sacred Lake.

Cecil is too self-conscious to play tennis in public because he does not play well. On principle he "despised the world as a whole", and yet he cannot help desiring the approval of others. "He never realised," the narrator tells us, "that it may be an act of kindness in a bad player to make up a fourth." In other words, Cecil's self-consciousness is unkind to the very persons whose good opinion he is uncomfortably desirous of acquiring. In dramatic contrast, George plays and plays to win. The simplicity of his desire endears him to Lucy.

Even though Cecil is self-conscious, self-thwarting, and uncomfortable in his own skin, Forster portrays him with considerable imaginative generosity. In *Middlemarch,* the "open, ardent" Dorothea Brooke marries the withholding and suspicious Casaubon. George Eliot, having described how Dorothea's youthful misperceptions have trapped her in a marriage devoid of direct intimacy and trust, famously stops mid-sentence to ask: *"why always Dorothea?"* – then turns to offer a sympathetic account of Dorothea's husband's parallel misperceptions and parallel unhappiness.

In similar fashion, *A Room With a View* offers a persuasive portrait of how Cecil conceives his mistaken attachment to Lucy. Cecil is a kind of intellectual, but he does not look for intellectual qualities in a wife. "Charm, not argument, was to be her forte," he complacently reflects. Instead, the basis of Cecil's attraction to Lucy is aesthetic. He admires Lucy as a work of art:

> *Italy worked some marvel in her. It gave her light, and – which he held more precious—it gave her shadow. Soon he detected in her a wonderful reticence. She was like a woman of Leonardo da Vinci's, whom we love not so much for herself as for the things that she will not tell us. The things are assuredly not of this life; no woman of Leonardo's could have anything so vulgar as a "story". She did develop most wonderfully day by day.*

# FIVE FACTS ABOUT
## *A ROOM WITH A VIEW*

### 1.

*A Room With a View* appeared in 1908, after *Where Angels Fear to Tread* (1905) and *The Longest Journey* (1907), though Forster conceived it first. Traces of its origins can be found in a notebook Forster kept during a tour of Italy he made with his mother (which inspired some of the characters and situations) in 1901-1902.

### 2.

In an early draft, George Emerson dies in a cycling accident after Mr Beebe prevents him from eloping with Lucy. Forster may have felt ambivalent about the published novel's ending, which finds George and Lucy together in Italy again. Novels should end on "a note of permanence", Forster said in his 1906 lecture, "Pessimism in Literature". However, modern life convinces us that "wedding bells" are but the "raising of the curtain for the play". In a realistic novel, only "separation" is permanent.

### 3.

Forster, who grew up in the shadow of Oscar Wilde's conviction for "indecency", never allowed his homosexuality to form the material of his published work. In 1911 his diary records "weariness of the only subject I both can and may treat — the love of men for women and vice versa". Forster showed friends his novel about the love between two men, *Maurice*, but did not publish it in his lifetime.

## 4.

The characters of *A Room With a View* have a life outside their novel. Forster sent a friend a parody of one of Wordsworth's "Lucy poems" about Charlotte Bartlett. He followed this with a letter purportedly from Charlotte, Lucy's "unattractive old cousin", and written in her characteristic martyred tones. Fifty years after his novel's publication, Forster impishly offered readers a glimpse at his characters' subsequent fates: George Emerson and Lucy remain in love, though displaced by the world wars; Cecil persists in mixing "culture and mischief", fabricating Belgian nationality for Beethoven so that his Moonlight Sonata can be played at a wartime party.

## 5.

*A Room With a View* is the only one of Forster's novels to have chapter titles: the detached, jocular tone of most of these (such as "Lying to Cecil") adds to the comic effect. But, significantly, the two chapters which form what Judith Herz calls the "pivots" in each section, chapters four and 12 – the murder in the piazza and the bathing scene at the Sacred Lake – have no titles, "suggesting that they belong to a different kind of novel, that they cannot be reduced to clever phrases in a satiric scheme".

In this passage she seems to him less a "living woman" than a beautiful and numinous eternal woman, whose mysteries can be contemplated by a true connoisseur like himself. Cecil echoes the famous description of Leonardo's Mona Lisa at the conclusion of Walter Pater's *Studies in the History of the Renaissance*:

> It is a beauty wrought out from within upon the flesh, the deposit, little cell by cell, of strange thoughts and fantastic reveries and exquisite passions... All the thoughts and experience of the world have etched and moulded there, in that which they have of power to refine and make expressive the outward form, the animalism of Greece, the lust of Rome, the mysticism of the middle age with its spiritual ambition and imaginative loves, the return of the Pagan world, the sins of the Borgias.

Aestheticism, the late 19th-century literary movement that took the sensuous appreciation of beauty in Pater's book as a touchstone, can become, Forster suggests, a damaging kind of asceticism. When Cecil asks to kiss Lucy for the first time, he ruins the moment for himself through excessive self-consciousness. His preoccupation with passion as an intellectual ideal quite forecloses actual passion. When the kiss fails to correspond to his aesthetic ideal of unrestrained passion, he is obliged to "recast the scene" more flatteringly in his mind.

Ultimately, Lucy realises that Cecil's aestheticism transforms her into an object, not an actor in her own right. In contrast, George tells her: "I want you to have your own thoughts even when I hold you in my arms."

Cecil is wrong about human relations but full of admirable opinions. He is both cultured and designing, qualities which might be expected to appeal to the novelist. Cecil is also intellectually opposed to snobbery and philistinism. Indeed, Forster delights in giving uncongenial opinions to sympathetic characters, and *vice versa*. He believed in the primacy of personal relations over politics and opinion. His novels resist easy moral accountancy. Mrs Honeychurch, one of the novel's more sympathetic characters, detests "literature in the hands of females" – an opinion hardly likely to be shared by Forster, friend of Virginia Woolf and devotee of Jane Austen. Lionel Trilling notes that the creation of "antagonistic principles is a game" and concludes that Forster "plays it only to mock it". Still, Cecil Vyse (Gothic) and George Emerson (Greek) represent distinct alternatives for Lucy: she spends the second half of the novel discovering how much she prefers the latter.

Mrs Honeychurch hopes that George Emerson and his father are "no relations of Emerson the philosopher, a most trying man". The Emersons, however, are spiritual, if not familial, relations of the philosopher. Ralph Waldo Emerson, the father of Transcendentalism, was extremely "trying" to the divines of 19th-century Christianity. He resigned as a Unitarian minister when he could no longer affirm Christian dogma. As a transcendentalist, Emerson stressed communion with nature and believed that truth is an ideal that can only be approached individually and passionately. "A mind might ponder its thought for ages," Emerson wrote, "and not gain so much self-knowledge as the passion of love shall teach it in a day." In Mr Beebe's study, Forster's Mr Emerson offers Lucy a very similar account of love and knowledge: "Passion does not blind. No. Passion is sanity, and the woman you love, she is the only person you will ever really understand."

Unlike R.W. Emerson, the Emersons of *A Room With a View* do not believe there is a transcendent meaning to the universe: "George and I both know... that all life is perhaps a knot, a tangle, a blemish in the eternal smoothness." Unlike his father, George at first finds this meaninglessness nearly unbearable. Before George meets Lucy, he is in a state of existential despair. If Cecil is "better detached", George prizes affection and connection; he suffers from the "old trouble; things won't fit". It is only his encounter with Lucy, and the possibility of passionate connection with her, that convinces him life is worth living.

# Music in *A Room With a View*

Lucy's instinctual selection of musical pieces expresses her preference for George over Cecil, even before she can articulate it to herself. Mr Beebe first recognizes Lucy's passionate inner vision in her triumphant performance of Beethoven. At the Bertolini, Mr Beebe concludes it is "too much Beethoven" that sends her out on the fateful visit to the Piazza Signoria in Chapter Four. Playing music both clarifies her desires and indirectly delivers her into the arms of George Emerson. Later in the novel, it also provides an index of her dissatisfaction. Lucy refuses to play Beethoven for Cecil in the disheartening atmosphere of Mrs Vyse's apartment. Instead she plays Schumann, music in which the "sadness of the incomplete... throbbed in its disjected phrases, and made the nerves of the audience throb".

If the melody Lucy associates with Cecil is "incomplete", "broken", nerve-rending, George's melody is just the opposite. It suggests mysterious consummation and harmony between human and natural forces. After their pivotal encounter with George in the Piazza Signoria, Lucy looks over the Arno whose "roar was suggesting some unexpected melody to her ears". The fight she sees, writes James Buzard, culminates in a grotesque and sexually suggestive image inflected by Lucy's "blank puzzlement and horror":

> *They sparred at each other, and one of them was hit lightly on the chest. He frowned; he bent towards Lucy with a look of interest, as though he had an important message for her. He opened his lips to deliver it, and a stream of red came out between them and trickled down his unshaven chin.*

Lifting her eyes as she swoons, Lucy sees "Mr George Emerson... looking at her across the spot where the man had been".

Citing details like the "trickle of blood", some critics detect Lucy's "symbolic loss of virginity" in her close encounter with violence. Yet in Forster's earliest draft of the novel, it is not Lucy who witnesses the murder, but a male protagonist (to whom Lucy remains romantically unattached). Moreover, to say that an event or object is "symbolic" of something too neatly dissipates the sense of "muddle" *A Room With a View* so effectively creates. The stabbing in the piazza, for all its sexual overtones, might well suggest the crossing of a more spiritual boundary. The scene's bleak violence also evokes the world of threats outside the confines of Lucy's set. Equally, it represents the radical separation of the social vexations of the Pension Bertolini from the melodramatic violence of the Italian street. Moreover, it could serve as a reminder to both Lucy

*E.M. Forster (1879-1970) working on the libretto of Benjamin Britten's new opera*
Billy Budd *on 15th October 1949*

and George of the true fleetingness of human life and its squandered opportunities for joy.

In short, the significance of events and objects in *A Room With a View* is not reducible to coded symbolic meanings any more than a symphony is reducible to its programme. Forster is interested in the deft *arrangement* of images and ideas, the titular room with a view being only the most obvious of these. Frank Kermode shows how these so-called *leitmotifs* (the word was originally used in opera to suggest recurring musical phrases) resonate on a minute level in the scene in the piazza through the repetition of seemingly ordinary words. Forster, Kermode writes,

...admitted to his interviewers that he had learned from the Wagnerian motifs, but his own rhythms, as he called them in *Aspects of the Novel,* are less obtrusive. You are not meant always to know whether they are intended or not.

The power of Beethoven's piano sonata draws Lucy out of the pension and into the piazza; there, Kermode argues, its effects are audible in the prose rhythms of Forster's description of the murder:

The words—"across", "happen", and, less conspicuously, "done" are a form of music, commonplace in themselves as unordered sound, but a tune, a phrase, an earworm... Somewhere behind their play is [Beethoven's] Opus 111...

In *A Room With a View,* resonances carry far. When Lucy discovers proof of George's sincere affection for her at Windy Corner, "her brain expanded the melody", as she recounts to herself his faithfulness. Finally when Lucy and George have consummated their love, they hear the coachman singing outside their window of "passion requited, love attained". Since they are listening by the river Arno, they hear the under-song of "a more mysterious love" identified with the melody of the river itself.

# What kind of novel is
# *A Room With a View*?

## *Edwardian or Modernist?*

E.M. Forster's work appears peculiarly traditional in comparison with the radical literary experiments of his contemporaries. The novelist Zadie Smith labels Forster "an Edwardian among the modernists". Indeed, Forster read, reviewed and praised the leading modernists of his era including Marcel Proust, D.H. Lawrence, James Joyce, and Virginia Woolf. Yet for all his enthusiasm for these literary revolutionaries, in his own work Forster refused to make similarly uncompromising demands upon his reader. He believed "the fundamental aspect of the novel is its story telling aspect". Unlike *Ulysses* (1922) and *Mrs Dalloway* (1925), in which Joyce and Woolf substitute the events of one ordinary day for a traditional plot, Forster always provides the satisfactions of "story telling". In "Mr Bennett and Mrs Brown", Woolf, Forster's close social and literary ally, classes him with modernist writers interested in finding new literary "tools" to evoke "the direct sense of the oddity and significance of some character". Still, she wrote, this investigation of consciousness was compromised by reliance on conventional novelistic technique; it "spoilt his early work".

Forster, despite his enthusiasm for the work of modernist writers, was less interested in revolution – Woolf's "new tools" – than in continuity. In *Aspects of the Novel*, he imagined the novelist's work as timeless:

> We are to visualize the English novelists not as floating down that stream which bears all its sons away unless they are careful, but as seated together in a room, a circular room, a sort of British Museum reading-room – all writing their novels simultaneously. They do not, as they sit there, think "I live under Queen Victoria, I under Anne, I carry on the tradition of Trollope, I am reacting against Aldous Huxley." The fact that their pens are in their hands is far more vivid to them... their sorrows and joys are pouring out through the ink.

Forster's belief in the essential simultaneity of all English novelists underlies his reliance on literary conventions. If literary history is not really a process of development, then a modern writer is welcome to employ the traditional features of the novel. Features like a courtship plot – whom will Lucy marry? – or an intrusive narrator – "She loved Cecil; George made her nervous; will the reader explain to her that the phrases should have been reversed?" – are as useful to him as to his literary forbearers.

On the other hand, Forster employs these traditional techniques to depict a changed world.

Like Jane Austen, Forster revels in the comic possibilities of mistaken first impressions. Lucy Honeychurch, like Elizabeth Bennet in *Pride and Prejudice*, learns the difference between apparent cultivation (Cecil Vyse and George Wickham) and true decency (George Emerson and Fitzwilliam Darcy) through falling in love.

Austen's comedy takes place in a rational, orderly, and knowable world. A hundred years later, however, it is no longer tenable to believe in a universe ticking along like intricate clockwork. In the fields of biology and psychology respectively, Darwin and Freud emphasised the determining power of unconscious forces and instinctual drives. Mr Emerson offers Lucy an up-to-date view of the universe, stressing its conspicuous lack of intelligible meaning:

*"I only know what it is that's wrong with him; not why it is."*

*"And what is it?" asked Lucy fearfully, expecting some harrowing tale.*

*"The old trouble; things won"t fit."*

*"What things?"*

*"The things of the universe. It is quite true. They don't... George and I both know this, but why does it distress him? We know that we come from the winds, and that we shall return to them; that all life is perhaps a knot, a tangle, a blemish in the eternal smoothness."*

Lucy, in an act of comic misrecognition, prescribes stamp collecting and a change of scene to cure George Emerson's existential dread. After George rescues Lucy by taking her into his arms, he suddenly realises that his passion for her can provide a meaning for his life. It takes Lucy longer to recognize that George's existential questioning resonates with her own unconscious yearning.

George's despair about the retreat of meaning from the world resonates through the modernist literature of the period. According to Pericles Lewis:

> The modernists generally saw the world as devoid of inherent significance. For them, the task of the artist was not to discover a pre-existent meaning, but to create a new meaning out of the chaos and anarchy of actual modern life.

Though erotic love cannot change the limitations of the human condition, it can help an individual, as Auden put it, "find the mortal world enough". While Forster's characters live in a modern world riven to fragments and devoid of intelligible meaning, Forster's novels manifest the traditional virtues of coherence and intelligibility.

# A comic novel?

Much of *A Room With a View* is written under the sign of what Forster calls "the Comic Muse". As a comic novelist, his method is less satire than the gentle cultivation of absurdities. Forster's targets are the foibles and pretentions of people who believe themselves to be right-thinking, morally refined and interested in culture. Charlotte Bartlett, for instance, has a particular genius for accumulating minor afflictions and a perverse desire to parade her self-sacrifice. She insists on giving up her seat to her younger and richer cousin Lucy:

> "*The ground will do for me. Really I have not had rheumatism for years. If I do feel it coming on I shall stand. Imagine your mother's feelings if I let you sit in the wet in your white linen." She sat down heavily where the ground looked particularly moist. "Here we are, all settled delightfully. Even if my dress is thinner it will not show so much, being brown. Sit down, dear; you are too unselfish; you don't assert yourself enough." She cleared her throat. "Now don't be alarmed; this isn't a cold. It's the tiniest cough, and I have had it three days. It's nothing to do with sitting here at all."*

Forster's comedy targets the manners and mores of his closest relations. He based Lucy Honeychurch, for instance, on his grandmother and Eleanor Lavish on the novelist Emily Spender, Stephen

Spender's aunt. Forster's family belonged to the Clapham Sect, a group of cultivated and prosperous reformers centred around the abolitionist William Wilberforce. According to Frank Kermode this group "established the ethics, the interests and the incomes of such minor descendants as E.M. Forster".

The ethics, interests and incomes of Forster's other sect, the bohemian intellectuals of the Bloomsbury group, do not escape his comic grasp either. Like Forster himself, Cecil is a literary young man whose stance as an intellectual radical is undermined by his inherited income and habit of travelling with his mother. "Cecil," the narrator writes, "had taken to affect a cosmopolitan naughtiness which he was far from possessing."

## A Bildungsroman?

A Bildungsroman is a novel of self-development. It traces a youthful protagonist's path toward an adult role and a fully realised personality. After Lucy shares a moment of intimacy with George, the narrator identifies the moment as a turning point in her journey, "a situation where character tells, and where childhood enters upon the branching paths of Youth".

At the beginning of the novel Lucy is eager to "develop". Acutely conscious of her youth, she is eager for both experience and knowledge. At first,

Lucy tries to accept and emulate her cousin Charlotte's notions of propriety. However, her encounters with the unconventional Emersons, who value sincerity over decorum, soon make her feel the limitations of her upbringing. "My dear," Mr Emerson tells her, "I think that you are repeating what you have heard older people say. You are pretending to be touchy; but you are not really." George Emerson's romantic overtures precipitate a crisis. Lucy is forced to distinguish between what she feels and what her upbringing has taught her to feel. "You warned me to be careful. And I – I thought I was developing," she tells Charlotte before fleeing from Florence and the Emersons.

In a Bildungsroman, the protagonist's development culminates in a defining choice between alternatives. Often, alternative social roles present themselves in the form of marriage proposals. Jane Eyre must choose between becoming Mrs St John Rivers (wife and helpmeet to a zealous missionary) or Mrs Edward Rochester (wife and helpmeet to the maimed master of Thornton Hall). In *A Room With a View,* Cecil's proposal offers culture and social position without intimacy. George, on the other hand, requires her to "break the whole of life" for the sake of requited passion. A third option, an independent life of "typewriters and latchkeys", means Lucy would "suffer and grow old" away from the man she loves.

# Why does Mr Beebe oppose the marriage of George and Lucy?

Mr Beebe is shaken by Lucy's decision to marry George Emerson. "I am more grieved than I can possibly express," he says: "lamentable, lamentable – incredible." Yet he recovers his composure in the brief space of time it takes for George's father to ask him the natural question: "What's wrong with the boy?" For Mr Beebe, lamentation and incredulity give way immediately to indifference: "he no longer interests me. Marry George, Miss Honeychurch. He will do admirably."

In the Pension Bertolini and at Windy Corner, Mr Beebe's aloof yet sympathetic interest in George and Lucy closely resembles the attitude of the narrator. Mr Beebe, we learn, was "somewhat chilly in his attitude towards the other sex". However, young Lucy's rapt, expressive piano playing interests him. To Mr Beebe, it suggests inner depths of feeling of which Lucy herself is as yet unaware. Similarly, it is Mr Beebe alone who attempts to introduce the Emersons to the other members of the Bertolini. It is Mr Beebe who bridges boundaries of class and manners. Why, then, does he resist their match so violently?

Lionel Trilling attributes Mr Beebe's attitude to Christianity's ancient enmity to "the holiness of direct desire". After Lucy breaks her engagement to Cecil, Mr Beebe hopes he can prevent her from ever marrying: "His belief in celibacy... now came to the surface and expanded like some delicate flower." In this view, Mr Beebe has chosen a life for himself "neither sensual nor sensational", and would choose the same for Lucy if he could. By the end of the novel, both Mr Emerson and Mr Beebe understand that George's love for Lucy is both "of the body" and reciprocated. They simply disagree about whether sexual attraction is a transcendent or depraved aspect of human nature.

Other critics foreground Forster's homosexuality in interpreting Mr Beebe's "inhuman" reaction to Lucy and George's union. *A Room With a View* may explicitly celebrate "the holiness of direct desire", yet Forster could only represent his own desires indirectly. For much of the novel, Lucy feels stifled, repressed. The titles of chapters 16, 17 and 18 find her "lying to" George, Cecil, Mr Beebe, Mrs Honeychurch, Freddy, and the servants. For these critics, Lucy's repression – her willingness to deceive herself and others about the true nature and object of her desire – parallels Forster's own inability to treat same-sex desire in his published novels. They find in Forster's female protagonist an indirect channel for erotic interest in men like George Emerson. In this account, moments like Lucy's arguably phallic vision of "a tower... throbbing in the tranquil sky", or the antic, joyful physicality of the men's bathing party at the "Sacred

Lake", give voice to unspoken homosexual desire within the explicit heterosexual love story.

Does Mr Beebe want George for himself? If Lucy and George marry, there can be no return to the high-spirited freedoms of the Sacred Lake. For Mr Beebe, there will be no "call to the blood and the relaxed will". By bringing about Lucy's decisive conversation with Mr Emerson, Charlotte Bartlett unconsciously affirms at once George and Lucy's union and love that is "of the body". But Mr Beebe, the narrator tells us, was "from rather profound reasons, somewhat chilly in his attitude towards the other sex..." He consciously stands apart from heterosexual erotic desire and resists George's participation in it; his lamentation over George's romantic success turns, almost immediately, to a lack of interest.

In a traditional novel, marriage marks the end of the interesting uncertainties of courtship. Such plots end when the protagonist's choice of romantic partner is no longer in doubt. Mr Beebe, in this respect, sides with the openness of an ongoing plot and against the closure signified by wedding bells. He resists marriage in general, and marriage founded on the joys of gratified desire in particular. Mr Beebe believes that "they that refrain do better". He remains interested in maiden ladies like the Miss Allens, perhaps, because their yearning after romance never ceases. "They will end by going round the world," he says. Thus, Mr Beebe's interest in Lucy persists so long as she remains in a "muddle", unable to realise her heart's simple imperative: she ought to marry the man she loves.

In his study of "Problems of Closure in the Traditional Novel", the critic D.A. Miller notes that even the novels of Jane Austen, which explicitly extol sound and final choices of romantic objects, feature plots that prolong romantic uncertainty and doubt as long as possible. Similarly, the narrator of *A Room With a View* extols the passionate honesty of a mind and heart fixed on their true object. "And the true point of *A Room With a View*," John Beer writes, is

> that there is a truth of the mind and a truth of the heart; both must take their part in the birth of true love, which unites the two of them, transforming them into a single, imaginative passion.

"Muddle", a word that recurs often in the novel, signifies confusion on this essential point. Lucy is muddled when she thinks she loves Cecil, and is nervous about George (when the truth is the reverse). And it is a muddle that nearly sends her to join the Miss Alans in Greece, instead of into the arms of George. Yet "muddle" is also the indispensable and interesting complexity of the narrative.

# FURTHER READING

**Works of E.M. Forster**
Forster, EM. *Aspects of the Novel.* (Abringer Edition). Ed.
Oliver Stallybrass. London: Edward Arnold, 1927; 1977.

Forster, EM. *The Lucy Novels: Early Sketches for* A Room
With a View. Ed. Oliver Stallybrass (Abringer Edition).
London: Edward Arnold, 1977.

Forster, EM. *A Room With a View.* Ed. Oliver Stallybrass.
(Abringer Edition). London: Edward Arnold, 1908; 1977.

Forster, EM. *Two Cheers for Democracy.* Ed. Oliver
Stallybrass. (Abringer Edition). London: Edward Arnold,
1951; 1972.

**Secondary Reading**
Beauman, Nicola. *Morgan: A Biography of E.M. Forster.*
London : Hodder & Stoughton, 1993.

Beer, John. *The Achievement of E.M. Forster.* London:
Chatto & Windus, 1962.

Bradshaw, David, ed. *The Cambridge Companion to E.M.
Forster.* Cambridge: Cambridge University Press, 2007.

Buzard, James. *The Beaten Track: European Tourism,
Literature, and the Ways to 'Culture', 1800–1918.* Oxford:
Oxford University Press, 1993.

Das, G.K. and John Beer. *E.M. Forster: A Human
Exploration.* London: Macmillan, 1979.

Emerson, Ralph Waldo. *Essays and Poems.* New York: Library of America, 1996.

Fillion, Michelle. *Difficult Rhythm: Music and the Word in E.M. Forster.* Urbana: University of Illinois Press, 2010.

Furbank, P.N. *E.M. Forster: A Life.* London: Secker & Warburg, 1977-1978.

Gardner, Philip, ed. *E.M. Forster: The Critical Heritage.* London: Routledge and Keegan Paul, 1973.

Genette, Gérard. *Narrative Discourse : An Essay in Method.* Trans. Jane E. Lewin. Ithaca: Cornell University Press, 1980.

Hulme, Peter and Tim Youngs, eds. *The Cambridge Companion to Travel Writing.* Cambridge: Cambridge University Press, 2002.

Kenner, Hugh. *Joyce's Voices.* Berkeley: University of California Press, 1978.

Kermode, Frank. *Concerning E.M. Forster.* London : Weidenfeld & Nicolson, 2009.

Lewis, Pericles. *The Cambridge Introduction to Modernism.* Cambridge: Cambridge University Press, 2007.

Medalie, David. *E.M. Forster's Modernism.* Houndmills, Basingstoke, Hampshire: Palgrave, 2002.

Mendelson, Edward. "Baedeker's Universe". *Yale Review.* 74 (Spring 1985): 386-403.

Meyers, Jeffrey. ""Vacant Heart and Hand and Eye": The Homosexual Theme in *A Room With a View*". *English Literature in Transition,* 1880-1920,13:3 (1970): 181-192.

Miller, D.A. *Narrative and Its Discontents : Problems of Closure in the Traditional Novel.* Princeton: Princeton University Press, 1981.

Moretti, Franco. *The Way of the World: The Bildungsroman in European Culture.* London: Verso, 1987; 2000.

Pater, Walter. *Studies in the History of the Renaissance.* Ed. Matthew Beaumont. Oxford: Oxford University Press, 1873; 2010.

Rosecrance, Barbara. *Forster's Narrative Vision.* Ithaca: Cornell University Press.

Smith, Zadie. *Changing My Mind: Occasional Essays.* London: Penguin, 2011.

Tambling, Jeremy, ed. *E.M. Forster (New Casebooks).* Houndmills, Basingstoke, Hampshire: Macmillan, 1995.

Trilling, Lionel. *E.M. Forster.* New York: New Directions, 1943; 1964.

Woolf, Virginia. *Mr. Bennett and Mrs. Brown.* London: Hogarth Press, 1924.

Wood, James. *How Fiction Works.* London: Jonathan Cape, 2008.

# CONNELL GUIDES TO
# LITERATURE

## Novels and poetry

*Emma*
*Far From the Madding Crowd*
*Frankenstein*
*Great Expectations*
*Hard Times*
*Heart of Darkness*
*Jane Eyre*
*Lord of the Flies*
*Mansfield Park*
*Middlemarch*
*Mrs Dalloway*
*Paradise Lost*
*Persuasion*
*Pride and Prejudice*
*Tess of the D'Urbervilles*
*The Canterbury Tales*
*The Great Gatsby*
*The Poetry of Robert Browning*
*The Waste Land*
*To Kill A Mockingbird*
*Wuthering Heights*

## Shakespeare

*A Midsummer Night's Dream*
*Antony and Cleopatra*
*Hamlet*
*Julius Caesar*
*King Lear*
*Macbeth*
*Othello*
*Romeo and Juliet*
*The Second Tetralogy*
*The Tempest*
*Twelfth Night*

## Modern texts

*A Doll's House*
*A Room with a View*
*A Streetcar Named Desire*
*An Inspector Calls*
*Animal Farm*
*Atonement*
*Beloved*
*Birdsong*
*Never Let Me Go*
*Of Mice and Men*
*Rebecca*
*Spies*
*The Bloody Chamber*
*The Catcher in the Rye*
*The History Boys*
*The Road*
*Vernon God Little*
*Waiting for Godot*

# NEW: HISTORY GUIDES

**The French Revolution**\* by David Andress
**Winston Churchill**\* by Paul Addison
**World War One** by Max Egremont
**The American Civil War** by Adam Smith
**Stalin** by Claire Shaw
**Nelson** by Roger Knight
**The Glorious Revolution** by Ben Wilson
**Russia and its Rulers** by Simon Dickson
**The Tudors** by Susan Doran
**Napoleon** by Adam Zamoyski
**From Addison to Austen** by Oliver Cox
**The US Civil Rights Movement** by Stephen Tuck
**The Rise and Fall of the Third Reich** by Caroline Sharples
**The Cold War** by Jeffrey Michaels

\* Available now. The rest of the selection above, and other titles, will be available shortly.

---

---

To buy any of these guides, or for more information, go to
**www.connellguides.com**
Or contact us on (020)79932644 / info@connellguides.com

First published in 2016 by
Connell Guides
Artist House
35 Little Russell Street
London WC1A 2HH

10 9 8 7 6 5 4 3 2 1

Picture credits:
p.13 © Everett / REX / Shutterstock
p.31 © Kurt Hutton / Stringer / Getty Images

A CIP catalogue record for this book is available from the British Library.
ISBN 978-1-911187-11-0

Design © Nathan Burton
Assistant Editors:
Brian Scrivener & Paul Woodward

www.connellguides.com